CUTTING
for all
Occasions

Marianne Perlot

FORTE PUBLISHERS

Contents

© 2002 Forte Uitgevers, Utrecht
© 2002 for the translation by the publisher
Original title: *Silhouetsnijden voor alle gelegenheden*

Second printing January 2003
ISBN 90 5877 202 0

This is a publication from
Forte Publishers BV
P.O. Box 1394
3500 BJ Utrecht
The Netherlands

For more information about the creative books available from Forte Publishers:
www.hobby-party.com

Publisher: Marianne Perlot
Editor: Hanny Vlaar
Photography and digital image editing: Fotografie Gerhard Witteveen, Apeldoorn, The Netherlands
Cover and inner design:
Studio Herman Bade BV, Baarn, The Netherlands

Preface

I wear out so many knives, but I always find it enjoyable to cut shapes in cards. People tend to find the cards without pictures the most attractive. Sometimes, the simplicity of attractively coloured card and the cut out shape are enough. The square stencils with four different small shapes are an enormous source of inspiration, because you can cut them in so many different ways. You can even combine the shapes with pictures and funny corner pictures.

Silhouet cutting is ideal for people who wish to make their own wedding or birth cards, because you can make the same card as many times as you wish. But also for those who want variation, a card with a simple cut out shape is a perfect basis for making something really special.

I have used both old and new patterns in this book.

Marianne

Good luck and have fun!

Techniques

Silhouet cutting

Silhouet cutting is a simple technique where you cut out the outline of figures or text from card using a silhouet stencil. You can cut out the outline of the figures or text straight from the stencil using a hobby knife, although I find it easier to first draw around the shapes with a propelling pencil, remove the stencil and then cut along the lines by hand. You can stick the stencil in place using 3M non-permanent adhesive tape. The advantage of using a propelling pencil is that the lead of the pencil is long and thin, so that you can always get into the smallest corners.

If you use a normal pencil, make sure the point is nice and sharp. First, cut out the inner lines of the figure and then the outer circumference.

To cut straight lines, it is a good idea to cut along the edge of a ruler.

Make sure to check the knife regularly, because a blunt knife will not make a nice cut.

3D cutting

The 3D pictures are made using two or three layers. Most cutting patterns are given in this book. Use a piece of 3D foam tape to stick the layers on top of each other.

If you use two layers, you can also create an extra effect by raising the first layer. If you only use one layer, also try to raise up this single layer.

For those who do not know what 3D cutting is, carry out the following: cut out the entire first picture and stick it on the card. For the second layer, do not cut out the parts of the picture that are in the background and stick this picture exactly on top of the first picture using small pieces of foam tape.

For the third layer, only cut out the part which is in the foreground and stick this exactly on top of the second picture using small pieces of foam tape. The cutting patterns are made for three layers, but you can also use two or even more than four layers if you wish. I always use 3M Montage tape, which can be recognized by its green checks.

You can cut this tape into very small pieces, it never sticks to the scissors and you can even stick it to your cutting mat and cut it into very narrow strips. The protective layer of tape is very easy to remove. You can also use silicon glue, if you prefer.

Squirt the glue into an injection syringe and place drops of glue on the back of the picture. Remember to always close the tube and the syringe.

1. Silhouet stencils and cutting sheets.

2. Draw the lines and cut them out.

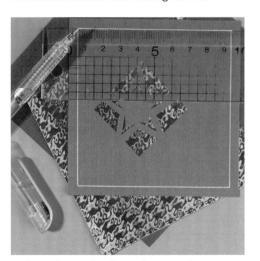

3. Draw decorative lines along a ruler.

4. Finish the card with 3D pictures.

You can push a nail into the opening of the syringe. If the glue does dry out, remove the dry glue from the back using the point of your scissors. You must always wait a couple of hours until the glue is dry enough to send the card.

The advantage of using glue is that you can puff up the picture (place the picture in the palm of your hand with the picture facing downwards and carefully rub the back of the picture with a pencil or a specially designed tool) or fold it upwards (a good example of this is the wings of a butterfly). You can also place the picture on top of the previous picture and slide it exactly into place whilst the glue is still wet. You cannot do this if you use tape.

Materials

- ❏ Card: P = Papicolor and A = Artoz (the colour numbers for both types of paper are given)
- ❏ Rainbow paper
- ❏ Corner and border silhouet cutting sheets
- ❏ Set of holographic paper
- ❏ Propelling pencil
- ❏ 3D cutting sheets
- ❏ Silhouet stencils
- ❏ 3D-tape, Scotch Montage tape (green checks)
- ❏ 3D scissors
- ❏ Cutting mat and hobby knife
- ❏ Non-permanent adhesive tape (Scotch Blue tape)
- ❏ Glitter glue

Card on the cover

What you need:
- ❏ Card: blue (P05 or P06/A427) and white (P30/A211)
- ❏ Snowman silhouet stencil
- ❏ Christmas border silhouet cutting sheet
- ❏ Silver holographic paper
- ❏ Ribbon

Make a blue double card (15 x 15 cm) by folding an A4 sheet double. Place the snowman stencil in the middle and cut it out. Stick holographic paper (15 x 11 cm) on the front of the blue card, against the line of the fold. If you cut out the snowmen according to the cutting pattern (see page 6), you will have at least two pictures left, which you can use to make gift labels.

Card on page 1

What you need:
- ❏ Card: black (P01/A219)
- ❏ Candle silhouet stencil
- ❏ Gold holographic paper
- ❏ Gold gel pen

Take a black card (12.5 x 12.5 cm or 13 x 13 cm). Cut the pattern out of the middle and draw a gold line around it.
Stick holographic paper with rays behind it. You can also easily tape over this pattern and make it rectangular. To do so, use non-permanent adhesive tape and draw around the pattern.

Cards with vellum

Silhouet cutting can combine really nicely with printed vellum.

What you need:
- ❏ *Card: dark red (P43/A519), dark pink (P33/A481), lavender (P31/A425) and white (P30/A211)*
- ❏ *Silhouet stencils: cat, rose, tulip, goose and butterflies*
- ❏ *A4 sheets of vellum (by Pergamano)*
- ❏ *Ribbon and hole punch*

The method is the same for all the cards. First, make a square double card (15 x 15 cm). It has been chosen to combine blue with white and red with cream. Cut a 15 cm wide strip lengthways off an A4 sheet. Place the stencil 0.5 cm or 1 cm from the right-hand side of the card. Stick down the stencil, draw around the figure and then cut it out. On the left-hand side of the card, score a line 2.5 cm from the figure's straight line which you have just cut out.

Fold the card over. You can now cut the front and back of the card to the same width. Cut the vellum lengthways through the middle. You now have two strips which you can use. Score the vellum 15 cm from the right-hand side and fold it over. In this way, you can cover the whole of the front of the card with vellum if you fold it around the card. Always be careful when scoring, because the pattern usually means that the vellum has a top and a bottom. There is sometimes an attractive border on the side which you can use in your design. Do not fold the vellum straight away, but place it between the square and the cut out card. You can now slide it to a position that you like and then score and fold it. Slide the three separate parts together and carefully hold them together. Use the hole punch to make holes through all three layers and tie an attractive ribbon through the holes. Many people who enjoy silhouet cutting already have these stencils. If so, you will not have to buy new stencils for these new designs. All you need are some A4 sheets of vellum. If you prefer not to use ribbons, you can glue the back of the separate pieces together.

Birth cards

The popular, fashionable colour of silver-grey is nowadays also found on birth cards.

What you need:
- ❏ *Card: cream (P03/A211) and silver-grey (A215) (the grey by Papicolor is too dark, so choose a pastel colour from the same collection)*
- ❏ *Birth silhouet stencil*
- ❏ *Ribbons and hole punch*
- ❏ *Light box and embossing tool*
- ❏ *BORN embossing stencil (EC 9726)*

All the cards are the same size: cut an A4 sheet of card lengthways through the middle and fold it double. For three cards, a bit is also cut off the top. Cut along the edge of a ruler. You can also place a pencil line on the card (on the back) and cut a border using figure scissors. Embossing is done as follows. Place the stencil on the front of the card in the place where you wish to have the embossed text or picture.

The text must be readable. Turn the stencil and the card over and place them on the light box. Next, accurately determine the position. Rub the area to be embossed with a candle (do not forget to first remove the wick) to make it easy to emboss. Use the tool to push the card through the opening in the stencil. Push it around the edge. Repeat it a number of times, if necessary, increasing the pressure each time.

1. Two ducks

Cut 2.5 cm off the card. Draw pencil lines 1.5 cm from the line of the fold and 1.5 cm from the edge of the card, and another line 2.5 cm from the bottom of the card. Cut out the ducks. Use a hole punch to make a small round hole in the neck and thread a ribbon through it. The white card is 1 cm shorter than the card itself.

2. A daughter

Cut 1.5 cm from the front of the card and stick pink transparent vellum in the card. You can print text on the vellum using your printer. Cut an opening (7.5 x 7.5 cm) in a scrap piece of strong card and use this to emboss a square window. Emboss the text in the bottom of the window. It is handy to first place the stencil on the card so that it is readable and then turn it over on the light box. You can now cut out the duck. Use a hole punch to make a small hole in the neck and thread a ribbon through it.

3. Duck on a blue background

Use the square which you made for card 2 to emboss a window. Make a white square (6 x 6 cm) and cut the duck out of it. You can also cut the duck out of a piece of scrap card first and then cut out the figure with a 1 cm border. Tie the ribbon. Next, stick the duck on blue card and cut this so that there is a 1 mm border. This method allows you to make the same card over and over again.

4. A grandchild

Grandmothers and grandfathers also like to receive a card of congratulations. Draw a pencil line 4.5 cm from the edge of the card and cut along the line using figure scissors. Emboss the text on a white rectangle (14 x 9.5 cm) and stick this on the inside of the card against the line of the fold.

Draw a checked pattern (1 x 1 cm) on the back of a piece of white card (8 x 8 cm), starting with the diagonals. Cut the duck exactly out of the middle of the checked pattern. Next, emboss a small heart from the embossing stencil on the cross points of the pencil lines and one or two dots on these lines between the hearts. You can use the dot of the i for the dots. You can also make a hole in thick card using a large or small hole punch and use this circle to emboss your pattern.

There are three other patterns on the silhouet stencil which you could use, but the duck is my favourite.

1.

2.

3.

4.

1.

2.

3.

Cat cards

Cards for both young and old. They are suitable for congratulating somebody, wishing somebody well or for no particular reason.

What you need:
❑ *Card: cream (P29/A211), orange-red (P11) or bright red (P12/A549) and grey (P44/A21)*
❑ *Cat silhouet stencil*
❑ *Cats cutting sheets 1 and 2 (AK 013 and 014)*

Children, in particular, enjoy to make these cat cards and to make a story using different pictures. Be careful when using a sharp knife.

1. Red cat

Cut 10 cm off an A4 sheet and fold the card double. Envelopes for this size card are available from supermarkets. Place the stencil on the inside of the card so that the distance from the left-hand side, the right-hand side and the bottom is the same. Cut out the cat. Cut a piece of cream card (9 x 16 cm) and stick this on the front of the card, also making sure the distance from the left-hand side, the right-hand side and the bottom are the same.

You will now see that a piece of orange-red card remains at the top of the card. Cut out one of the cats which uses two paws to look over something. You can now write your message on the front of the card.

Next, cut a strip of cream card (9 x 14 cm) and stick this on the inside of the card. Decorate the card as you wish with cats and cat toys.

The heads of the cats and some paws are made 3D. The first layer has been stuck on the card using 3D tape and so have all the single layer pictures.

2. Grey cat

Accurately cut the stencil out of grey card. Use the outer edges of the stencil as a line to cut along. Cut a 10 cm wide strip off an A4 sheet of cream card and fold it double.

Stick the cut out grey cat to the inside of the card. Draw two straight lines with a pencil in a corner and use these lines to stick cats, grass and flowers on. The heads of the cats and the flowers are made 3D. Use a fine-liner to draw an imaginary flight movement for the butterfly.

3. White cat

Cut a 16 cm wide strip lengthways off an A4 sheet of cream card. Score fold lines 9.7 cm from both the outer edges. Place the cat stencil exactly in the middle and copy the figure. Cut out the cat.

Cut an orange-red strip (9 x 15 cm) and stick this behind the cut out cat. Fold the card closed so that this is on the front of the card. Stick a cat on the card and write a wish on the front. Place a ruler parallel to the cut out straight line at the bottom of the cat and draw a line to the left-hand and right-hand sides, which stops 1cm from the edge of the card. Also draw a horizontal line 1 cm from the edge. Decorate the card with cat pictures. Make the heads of the cats and the flowers 3D. Stick the single layer pictures on the card with 3D tape. Stick a small strip of tape under the bodies of the butterflies and fold the wings upwards.

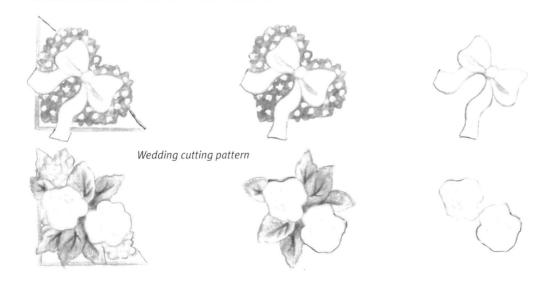

Wedding cutting pattern

Wedding cards

Cream and green is a colour combination which goes well with the romantic corner pictures.

What you need:
- ❏ *Card: creamy yellow (101) and green (474) (both Canson Mi-Teintes) and gold*
- ❏ *Marriage and rose silhouet stencils*
- ❏ *General corner silhouet cutting sheet*
- ❏ *Glitter glue and gold gel pen*

1. Dove

Start with a cream card (15 x 15 cm), followed by a gold card (11.5 x 11.5 cm), a green card (11 x 11 cm) and a cream card (10 x 10 cm). Cut the dove exactly in the middle and draw a gold square around the dove 2 cm from the cut out figure using a gel pen.
Stick 3D corner pictures in all the corners. Also draw a decorative line in the middle of the green border which sticks out from under the cream square. Add plenty of festive glitter glue to the roses.

2. Marriage card

Start with a coloured card (15 x 15 cm). Cut an A4 sheet through the middle and fold one half double. Place the rose stencil exactly in the middle and cut it out. Draw a decorative line and stick corner pictures on the card.

3. Collage card

Start with a cream card (15 x 15 cm), followed by a green square (13 x 13 cm). Next, cut out four cream squares (6 x 6 cm). Cut a pattern out of two of these squares. Cut out another two green squares (5 x 5 cm) and draw decorative lines. Stick pieces of gold card behind the cut out patterns and stick the small squares on the large square and then stick this on the card. Make the corner pictures 3D. Finally, draw another decorative line on the white card close to the green square.

4. Hearts

Cut out a cream card (15 x 15 cm) and three rectangles (green 13 x 9.5 cm, gold 12 x 8.5 cm and cream 11.5 x 8 cm). Draw decorative lines on the cream and green rectangles. Cut the picture exactly out of the middle. Stick the different layers on the card. Stick the corner pictures on the card and add glitter glue.

Christmas goose

With this goose (my favourite from part 1), you can make excellent Christmas cards.

What you need:
- ❏ Card: dark red (P43/A519), bright red (P12/A517), Christmas green (P18/A339) and cream (P29/A211)
- ❏ Goose silhouet stencil
- ❏ Silhouet cutting sheet with Christmas borders and corners
- ❏ Ribbon and glitter glue
- ❏ Gold border stickers

Give the cards an extra touch with glitter glue.

1. Poinsettia

Place the stencil on a strip of cream card. Place non-permanent adhesive tape over it 7 cm from the straight, horizontal line on the top of the stencil. Only cut out the top of the goose. The borders around the goose are 1.5 cm. Stick the goose on a green square (10 x 10 cm) and stick this on a dark red card (13 x 13 cm).

Add stickers around the border and finish the border with white 3D poinsettias.

2. Borders with Christmas decorations

Cut out a bright red card (15 x 15 cm), a green card (15 x 12 cm) and a cream card (15 x 11 cm). Cut the goose exactly out of the middle. Tie a ribbon around the neck and stick everything on the card. Stick the sticker strips on the green card and make the Christmas decoration border 3D.

3. Christmas holly

Take a green card (15 x 15 cm) and a bright red card (11 x 15 cm). Stick the bright red card on the front of the card, against the line of the fold. Cut a 15 cm wide strip off an A4 sheet of cream card and place the goose stencil 0.5 cm from the right-hand side. Copy the goose and cut it out. Next, score a line 1.5 cm from the cut out straight line in the goose figure and fold the card over. Stick the back against the green/red card. Draw a decorative line along the red

border and stick the border sticker on the card. Make the holly border 3D.

4. Goose in a circle

Cut out a white square (10 x 10 cm). Place the goose in the middle and only cut out the outline (see photograph). The diameter of the circle is 6.8 cm.

Draw decorative lines around the white card, close to the edge. Cut a circle (Ø 8 cm) out of the red card (13 x 13 cm) and stick the white card on this. Stick green card (10 x 10 cm) inside the card. You can use this to write your Christmas message.
Stick the corner pictures against the gold lines and make them 3D.

Christmas cards

Red and green will always

be warm Christmas colours.

These combine excellently with

gold and the corner pictures.

What you need:
- ❏ *Card: dark green (P18/A309)*
  and bright red (P12/A549)
- ❏ *Christmas silhouet stencil*
- ❏ *Christmas corner silhouet*
  cutting sheet

1. Three Christmas trees

Cut 10 cm off an A4 sheet and fold the card double. Draw pencil lines 3 cm from the fold and the edge of the card. Next, draw a pencil line 3 cm from the top and bottom of the card. Cut the bottom and top Christmas trees exactly in these positions. Next, draw a pencil line 17 mm from the patterns which you have just cut out to mark the exact location where you can cut out the final tree. Stick gold holographic paper behind the trees and decorate them with a couple of stars.

2. Christmas bears

Take a red card (13 x 13 cm), a gold card (12 x 12 cm) and a green card (11 x 11 cm). Use diagonal lines to determine the middle of the green card and cut out a star slightly above the middle point.

3. Christmas stockings

Cut a 10 cm wide strip off an A4 sheet of card and cut out the Christmas tree from the strip that remains (14 x 5 cm). Cut out two red squares (4 x 4 cm) and a rectangular strip (15 x 6 cm). Stick gold holographic paper (4.5 x 4.5 cm) behind the cut out Christmas tree and stick everything together. Draw a gold line on the green card close to the red squares. Stick 3D corner pictures in the corners of the card.

4. Birds

Start with a red card (13 x 13 cm), followed by a gold square (11 x 11 cm) and a green square (10 x 10 cm). Draw a pencil line 7 mm from the outer edge. Cut out the star in the top left-hand corner and cut out the Christmas tree in the bottom right-hand corner. Place the line to be cut exactly against the pencil line. Cut out red squares (4 x 4 cm) and stick 3D corner pictures on the card (see page 24).

Villages in the snow

Try to make a snowy winter village with these stencils, white card and glitter glue.

What you need:
- ❏ *Card: light lavender blue (P20/A425 or 150 (Canson Mi-Teintes), dark lavender blue (P31/A427), dark blue (P41/A417) and white (P30/A211)*
- ❏ *Blue tinted rainbow paper*
- ❏ *Christmas and snowy village silhouet stencils*
- ❏ *Silver and purple holographic paper*
- ❏ *Glitter glue*

1. Village

Cut a 10 cm wide strip off an A4 sheet of dark blue card and fold the remaining piece double. Cut a semicircle (Ø 14 cm) out of a sheet of blue rainbow paper. Tear a couple of hills from some 5 cm wide strips of card: one for the right-hand side of the card and one for the left-hand side of the card. Cut out part of the stencil (see the photograph). Stick everything on the card and add glitter glue for snow.

2. Church

Cut a 10 cm wide strip off an A4 sheet of lavender blue card and fold the remaining piece double. Cut out two strips (21 x 7 cm and 21 x 6 cm) from dark blue card and rainbow paper. Copy the church from the stencil with the four different figures.

Do not draw the bottom, but remove the stencil and draw the bottom yourself, making sure that the scene is 7 cm wide. You can also stick it on the card and then cut off the parts which stick over the edge. Cut the star out of the top of the rainbow paper. There is some excellent purple holographic paper with little squares and if you cut one out a bit bigger, it will fit behind the star. Stick everything on the card and add glitter glue for snow.

The set of holographic paper also contains pretty silver and gold paper, which will be used later in this book.

3. Village in a circle

Start with a square card (13 x 13 cm), followed by a light lavender blue circle (Ø 10 cm) and a dark lavender blue circle (Ø 9 cm).

Cut a circle (Ø 8 cm) out of blue rainbow paper. Cut a part of the pattern of the large stencil and stick this on the blue rainbow paper.

Cut everything away which does not fit in the circle.
Stick the layers on top of each other and add glitter glue to the edges of the roofs for snow.

4. Rectangular card with a star

This is a variation to card 2. Cut a 10 cm wide strip off an A4 sheet, fold the remaining card double and then make the card 1 cm shorter. Cut out a strip of blue rainbow paper (7 x 16 cm) and a strip of dark blue card (8 x 17 cm). Cut a part of the stencil with the snowy village so that it is 7 cm wide. Stick this on the blue rainbow paper and cut off the bits which stick over the edge. Only cut out the inner part of the star from the square stencil. Stick silver holographic paper with a fine pattern behind this. Make the snow glisten in the light of the star.

5. Christmas card with little squares

This white card is also long and narrow. Therefore, cut 10 cm off an A4 sheet of card. Draw pencil lines in the bottom left-hand and right-hand corners, which are 2 cm from the sides and the bottom of the card. Use these corners to cut out the church and the Christmas tree. You can position the star exactly between the two figures or at an angle as shown in the photograph. Cut out three squares with a border from the purple holographic paper with squares. Stick them straight or at an angle (for the star) behind the openings.

Add glitter glue and try to continue the lines by the square, as for the points of the star and the point of the church steeple. You can also continue the horizon with glitter glue.

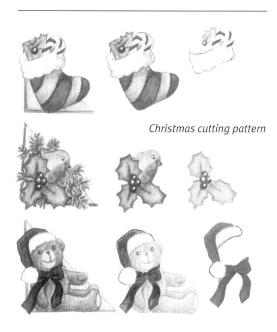

Christmas cutting pattern

Stars and Christmas

If you could see all the home-made Christmas cards I have received, you would see that blue is the most popular colour.

What you need:
❑ *Card: dark blue (P41/A417)*
    and gold card/holographic paper
❑ *Christmas decorations and*
    Christmas silhouet stencils
❑ *Gold gel pen*
❑ *Stickers with a Christmas text*

1. Gold Christmas decorations

Fold half an A4 sheet double. Use non-permanent adhesive tape to tape over the stencil 10 cm from the top straight line of the pattern (not from the top of the stencil). Copy the pattern on gold card and cut it out. Leave a border (approximately 2 cm) around the pattern.
Place this on the front of the card and mark the corner points. Connect these points together using a ruler and then cut out a rectangle which is 2 mm wider on all the sides than the rectangle which you have just drawn.
If you stick the cut out Christmas decorations behind the opening, a narrow gold border will be visible.

2. Card with four stars

Take a card (15 x 15 cm) and mark the middle point using a horizontal and vertical line. Draw pencil lines 0.5 cm from both sides of the two lines to make a 1 cm wide horizontal bar and a 1 cm wide vertical bar. Place the stencil exactly against the corners. Make sure the straight edges to be cut out of the stencil fit exactly along the bars which you have just drawn. For the card in the photograph, the stencil has been rotated clockwise, although you can also cut all the stars out straight or use a different pattern. Finish the card by drawing gold decorative lines. A piece of gold card behind the opening gives the card an extra finishing touch.

3. Star cards

Take a card (15 x 15 cm) and cut 7 cm from the front right-hand side. Draw lines 1 cm from this edge and 1 cm from the top and bottom edges. Cut out two stars in these corners and cut out the third star between them. For the card in the photograph, the inner parts of the star have not been cut out and a sticker has been stuck on the star instead. Stick a strip of gold holographic paper behind the card and use a gold gel pen to draw two lines 0.5 cm from the lines which have been cut. There is space to write a Christmas wish on the right-hand side.

4. Blue Christmas decorations

For card 1, you taped over the stencil 10 cm from the top of the card. You can also place this stencil on the front of this card, copy it and cut it out. Decorate the Christmas decorations with some star stickers and stick holographic paper behind the opening.

Gift label

When you tidy up, make it a habit to cut gift labels from all the scrap pieces of card. Stick the remaining pictures on the labels so that you always have some spare labels and never have small pieces of card which you no longer use.

Winter cutting pattern

1.

2.

3.

4.

1.

2.

3.

4.

Winter

Pretty, classic Christmas

scenes, which are fun to

make and nice to receive.

What you need:
- ❏ *Card: white (P30/A211) and olive green (P45)*
- ❏ *Blue tinted rainbow paper*
- ❏ *Snowman and Christmas tree*
  silhouet stencils
- ❏ *3D cutting sheets (Wild in the Winter - 3D 382,*
  Forest Animals - 3D 383,
  Snow Fun with suitable background - 3D 385,
  Winter Landscape - 3DA 3303 and
  Winter Forest 3DA 3302,
  as well as Christmas texts)

You can make the same type of card a number of times using the remaining pictures on the cutting sheets. You can really use everything.

Square cards (cards 1 and 4)

Take a card (15 x 15 cm) and place the stencil 0.5 cm from the line of the fold.
Cut out the figure. Stick a background inside the card and decorate the card with suitable pictures. You can also make these pictures 3D according to the cutting pattern. Do not forget to use glitter glue to make the snow glisten. You can also use the horizontal background from the cutting sheet. In that case, tape over the bottom part of the Christmas tree and the snowman and cut out a part of the picture that is 8 cm long to give a totally different effect.

Rectangular cards (cards 2 and 3)

This type of card (cut 10 cm off an A4 sheet of card and fold it double) is excellent to use. Place the snowman on the front of the white card, making sure that the borders on the bottom and sides are the same width. Cut out the snowman and stick blue tinted rainbow paper behind the opening. There are a lot of Christmas texts on the cutting sheet, so you can make at least five cards. The same is true for the green card. Cut an opening (6 x 13 cm) in the card. This can be easily done by drawing a pencil line on the back 3 cm from the top, 4 cm from the bottom and 2 cm from the sides. Draw a decorative line 0.5 cm from the edge of the opening. Cut out the snowman and cut it out of the frame. Stick it on the inside of the card using 3D tape.

Mourning cards

Everybody who receives a

home-made card during

a time of difficulty will

value it even more.

What you need:
- ❏ *Card:*
  black (P01/A219),
  cream (P03)
  and grey (A215)
- ❏ *Brown tinted rainbow paper*
- ❏ *Condolence silhouet stencil*
- ❏ *Silhouet corner cutting sheet*
  General
- ❏ *Gold gel pen*

pattern remains a bit stronger. Add a decorative line a couple of millimetres from the cut out pattern using a gel pen and a ruler. Decorate the card with some 3D flowers.

Fold an A4 sheet double. Place the stencil exactly in the middle and copy the figure.
In the black card, the whole pattern has been cut out. In the grey card, the flower has not been cut out and the straight lines of the cross have been continued.
For the cream card, these lines are not drawn all the way to the bottom, so that the cut out

I always choose a large card, because this gives you extra space to write something personal. A personal message is always valued during difficult times. If you find it difficult to write what you feel, look in a book of poems. You will find many texts which you can use.

The materials used can be ordered by shopkeepers from:
Kars & Co. B.V., Ochten, the Netherlands